Letterland®

PICTURE DICTIONARY

Devised and written by Richard Carlisle

Educational Editor: Lyn Wendon

Collins Educational

An imprint of HarperCollinsPublishers

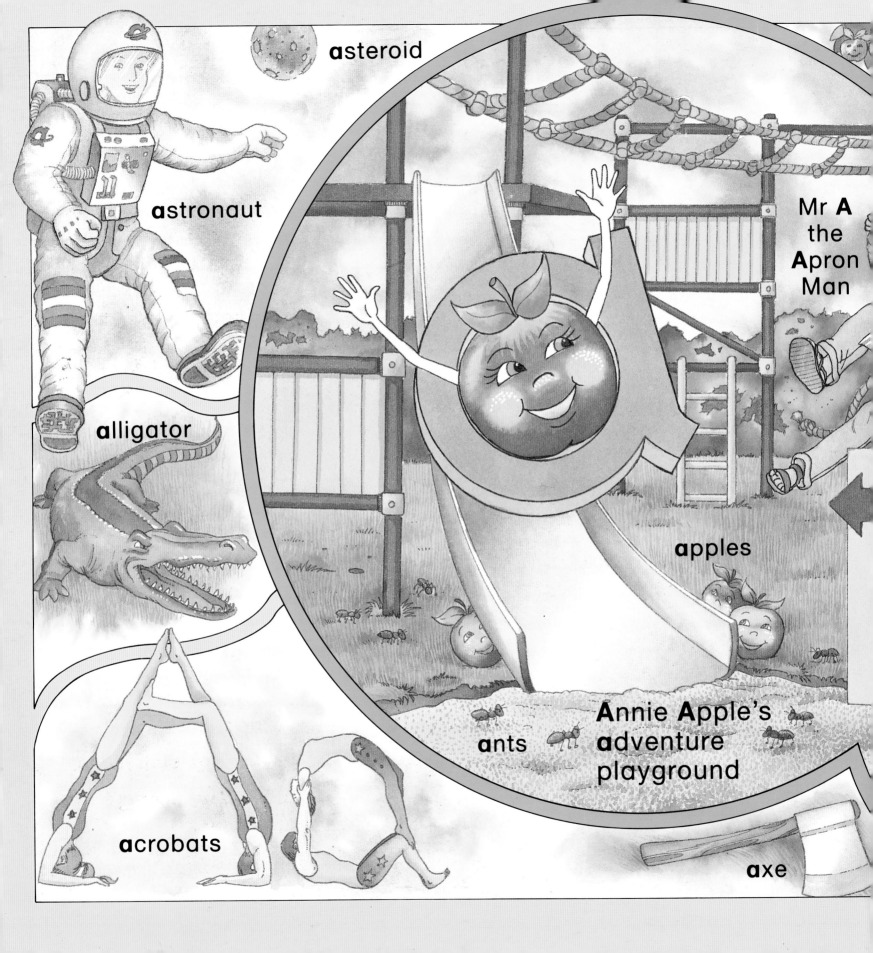

asteroid

astronaut

alligator

acrobats

Mr **A** the **A**pron Man

apples

Annie **A**pple's **a**dventure playground

ants

axe

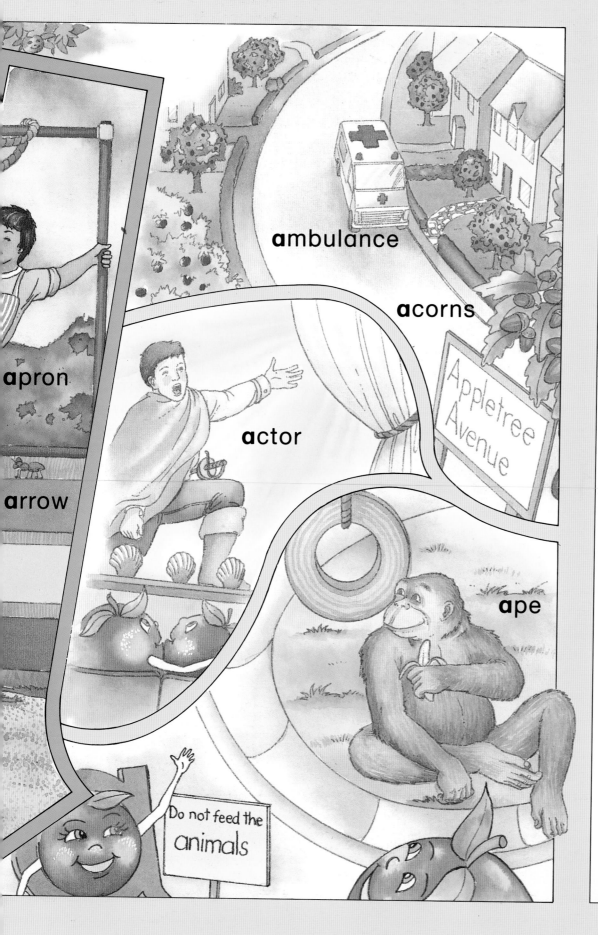

ambulance

acorns

apron

actor

Appletree Avenue

arrow

ape

Do not feed the animals

Aa

Find the word

acrobats	apples
actor	Appletree
adventure	arrow
alligator	asteroid
ambulance	
animals	astronaut
Annie	Avenue
ants	axe
Apple	

Mr A

acorns	apron
ape	

Activities

Add up all the apples.

Add up all the ants.

Find an angry animal.

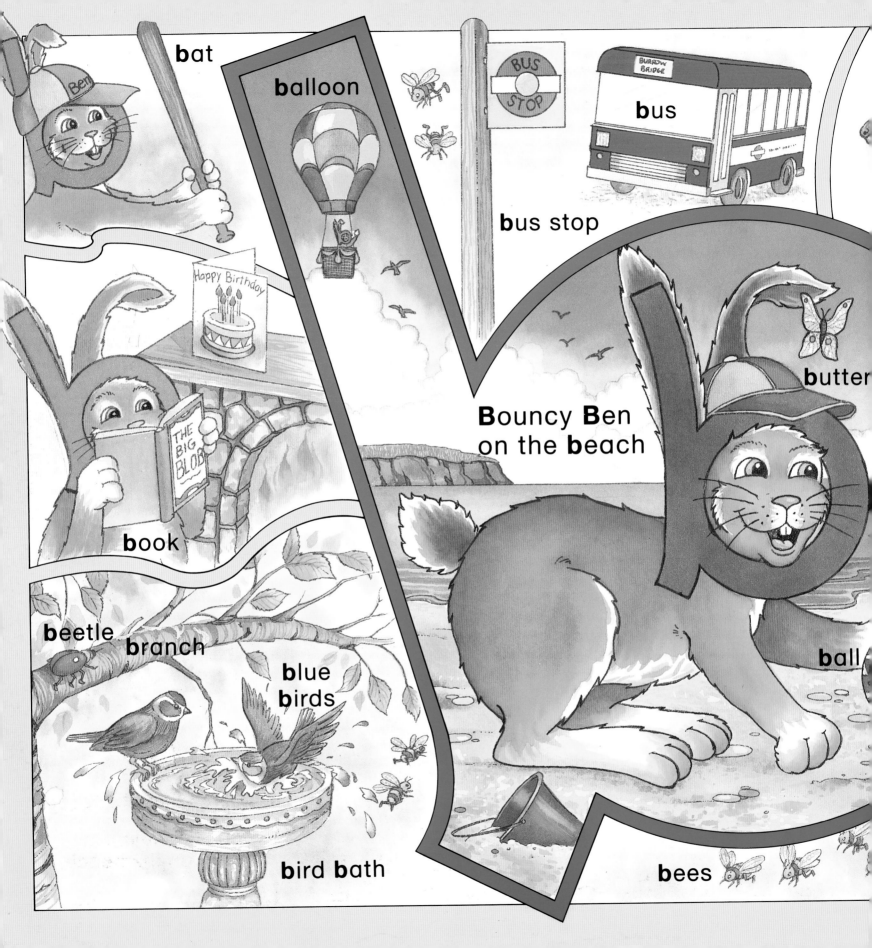

bat

balloon

bus

bus stop

book

beetle **b**ranch

blue **b**irds

bird **b**ath

Bouncy **B**en on the **b**each

butter...

ball

bees

bear

breakfast in **b**ed

blanket

boat

bottle

butter

baked **b**eans

brown **b**read

bridge

bicycle

BANG!

Bb

Find the word

baked	**B**irthday
ball	**b**lanket
balloon	**B**LOB
BANG!	**b**lue
bat	**b**oat
bath	**b**ook
beach	**b**ottle
beans	**B**ouncy
bear	**b**ranch
bed	**b**read
bees	**b**reakfast
beetle	**b**ridge
Ben	**b**rown
bicycle	**b**us
BIG	**b**us stop
bird	**b**utter
birds	**b**utterfly

Activities

Count all the bees.

Find something buried on the beach.

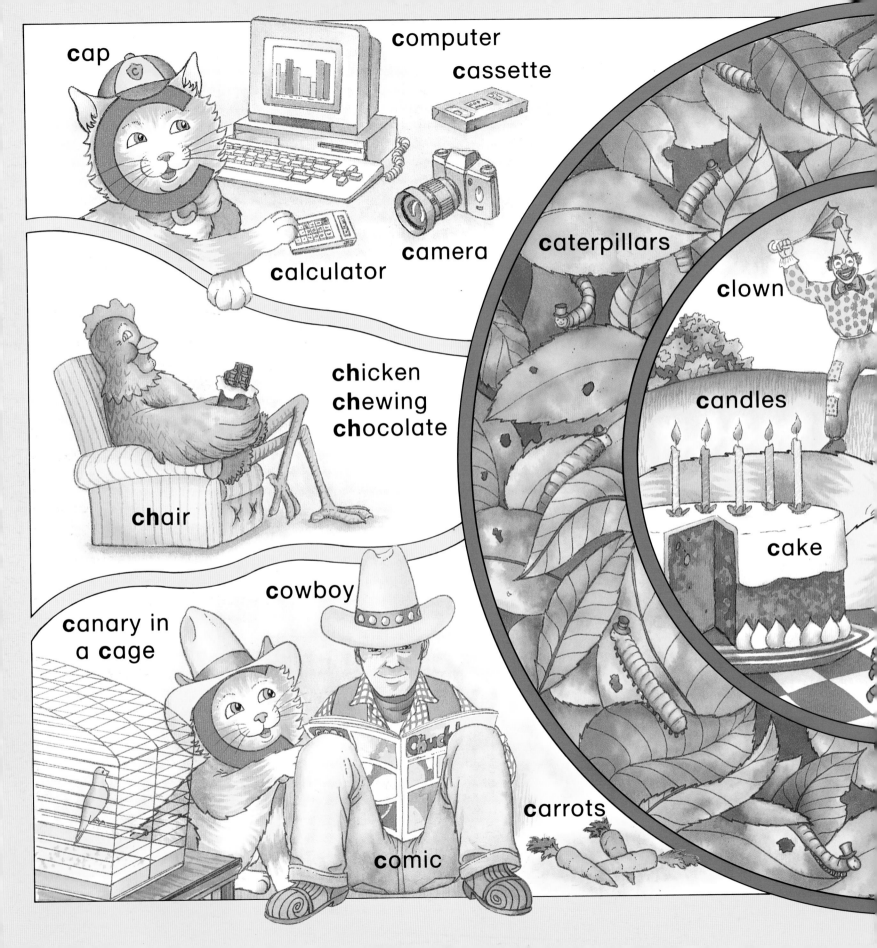

cap

computer

cassette

camera

calculator

caterpillars

clown

candles

cake

chicken
chewing
chocolate

chair

cowboy

canary in
a cage

comic

carrots

clock covered
in cobwebs

crow

Clever Cat's
picnic

church

camel

aws

crab

crane

crate

car

Find the word

cage
cake
calculator
camel
camera
canary
candles
cap
car
carrots
cassette
Cat
caterpillars
chair
chewing
chicken

chocolate
church
Clever
claws
clock
clown
cobwebs
comic
computer
covered
cowboy
crab

crane
crate
crow

Activities

Find all the
caterpillars.

Count the candles
on Clever Cat's
cake.

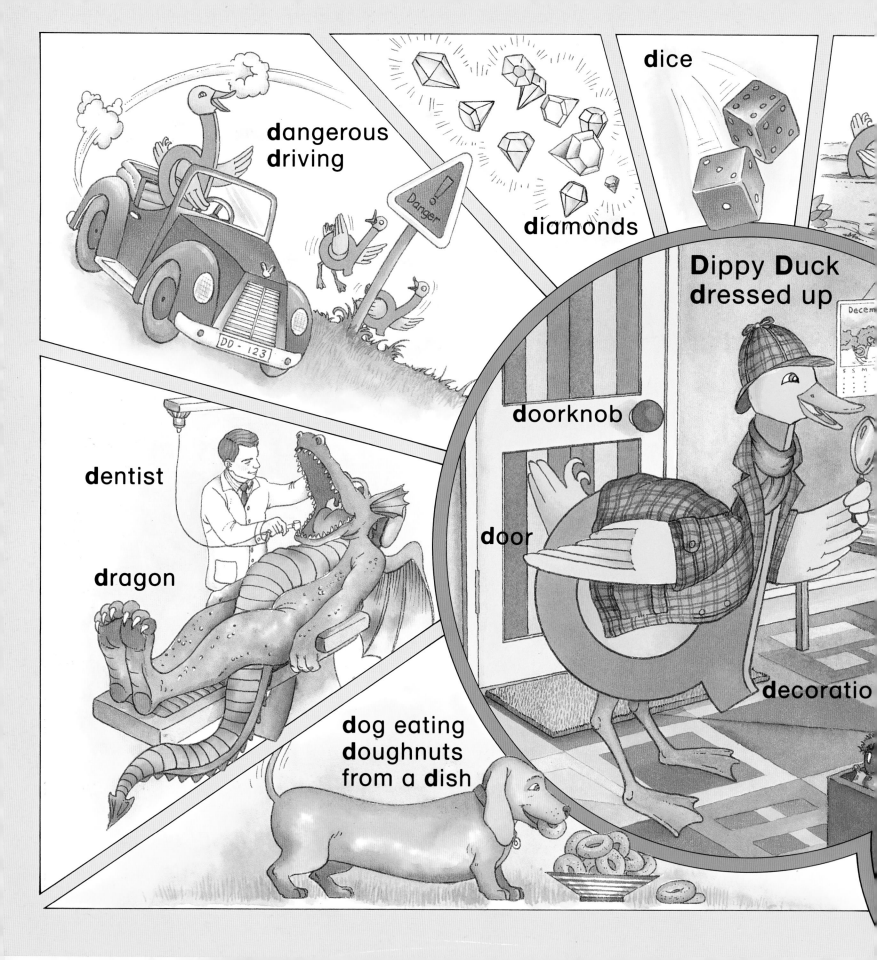

dangerous driving

diamonds

dice

dentist

dragon

dog eating doughnuts from a dish

Dippy Duck dressed up

doorknob

door

decoratio

December

affodils

dartboard

Doctor in a **d**eckchair

DO NOT DISTURB

diving **d**olphins

lesk

doll

drum

drumsticks

Which **d**oor is **d**ifferent?

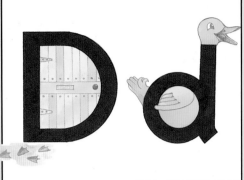

Dd

Find the word

daffodils	**D**O
Danger!	**D**octor
dangerous	
dartboard	**d**og
December	**d**oll
deckchair	**d**olphins
decorations	
dentist	**d**oor
desk	**d**oorknob
diamonds	**d**oughnuts
dice	**d**ragon
different	**d**ressed
Dippy	**d**riving
dish	**d**rum
DISTURB	**d**rumsticks
diving	**D**uck

Activities

Add up the dots on the dice.

Find the dove.

Count the ducks.

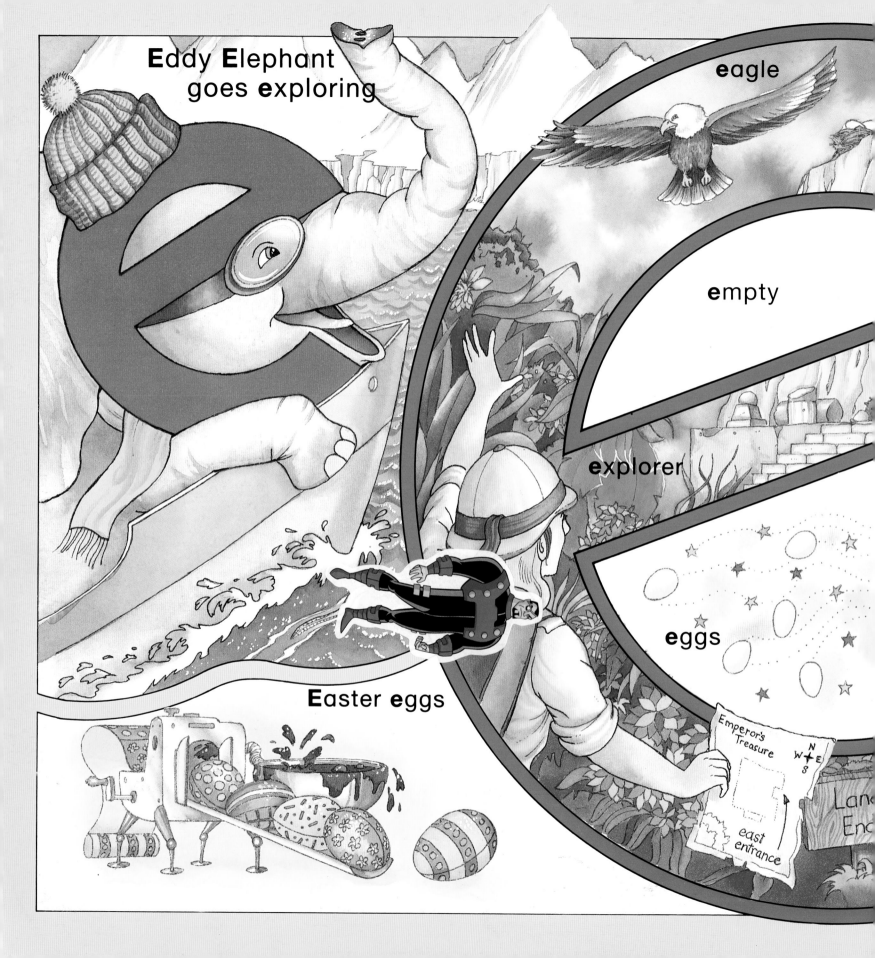

Eddy **E**lephant goes **e**xploring

eagle

empty

explorer

eggs

Easter **e**ggs

Emperor's Treasure

east entrance

Lan
En

E e

envelope

E. Elephant
11 Elmtree Estate
Letterland

escalator

entrance

EXIT

Mr E the
Easy
Magic
man

explosion

Eddy Elephant
eating eclairs

Find the word

eclairs	entrance
Eddy	envelope
eggs	escalator
Elephant	Estate
Elm	EXIT
Elmtree	explorer
Emperor	exploring
empty	explosion
End	

Mr E
eagle   Easy
east   eating
Easter

Activities

Add up all the eggs.

Find whose treasure
is on the map.

Find the hidden eel.

Fireworks with **F**ireman **F**red

fence

fox

fireflies i
the fores

funny fa
on a flag

factory

fie

frog

fern

football

FIRST AID

fifty pence

fire engine

frog

farm   **f**armer

Find the word

face	**F**ireworks
factory	**F**IRST AID
farm	flag
farmer	football
fence	forest
fern	fork
fields	fox
fifty pence	**F**red
fire engine	frog
fireflies	funny
Fireman	**F**ulham

Activities

Count the fireflies.

Count the foxes in the field.

Find a hidden fish.

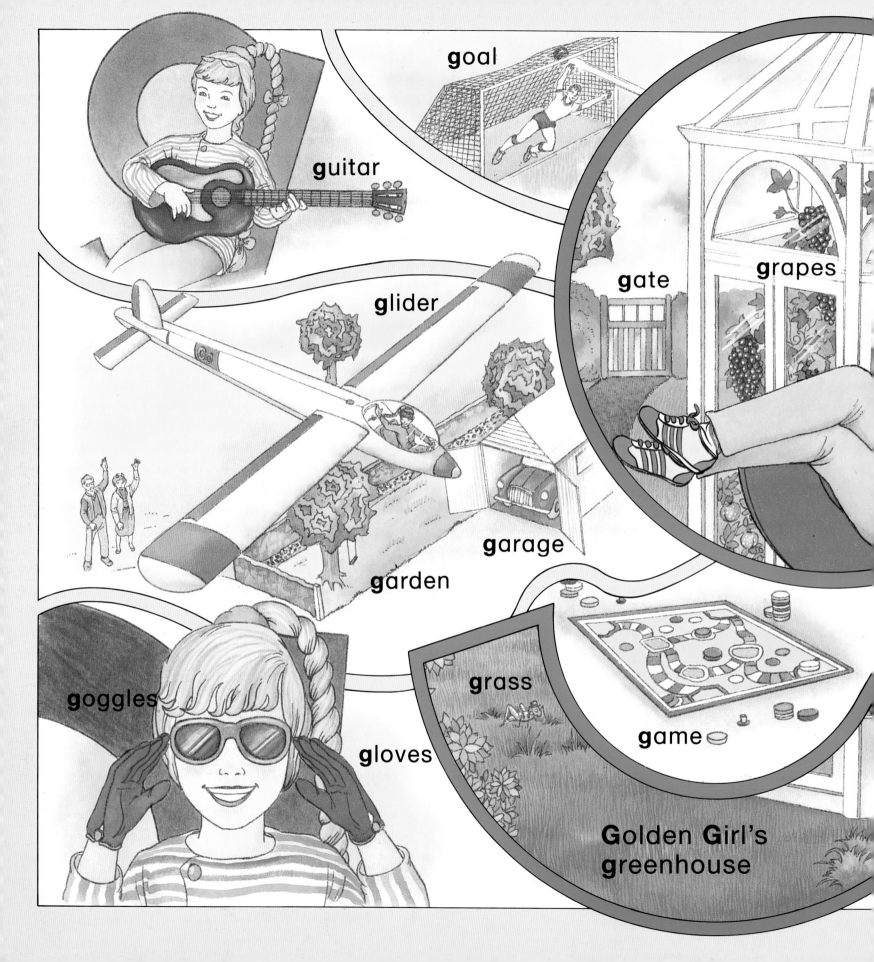

guitar

goal

gate

grapes

glider

garage

garden

goggles

grass

gloves

game

Golden **G**irl's
greenhouse

glass

glasses

gorilla

granny
and
grandad

goat
grazing

goose

ghost

go kart

Find the word

game	**g**oggles
garage	**g**o kart
garden	**G**olden
gate	**g**oose
ghost	**g**orilla
Girl	**g**randad
glass	**g**ranny
glasses	**g**rapes
glider	**g**rass
gloves	**g**razing
goal	**g**reenhouse
goat	**g**uitar

Activities

Count the animals.

Find the grasshopper.

Find the green grapes.

The **H**airy **H**at Man at **h**ome

hatstand

hair

hand

hill

hamburger

honey

Home Sweet Home

hat

horse

holl...

HOTEL

helmet

Hilltop Hotel

hip...

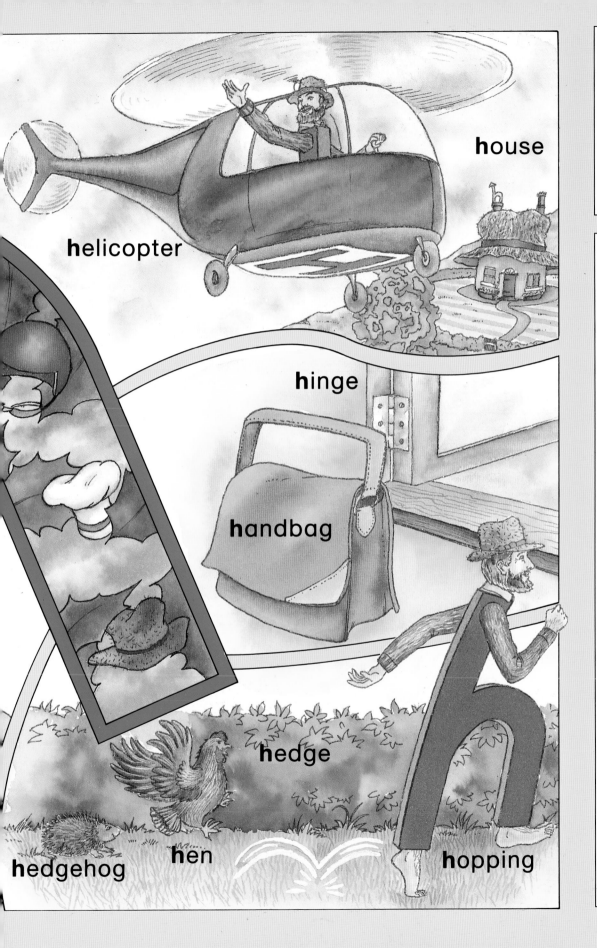

house

helicopter

hinge

handbag

hedge

hedgehog

hen

hopping

Find the word

hair	**h**ill
Hairy	**H**illtop
hamburger	
hand	**h**inge
handbag	**h**ippo
hat	**h**olly
hatstand	**h**ome
hay	**h**oney
hedge	**h**opping
hedgehog	**h**orse
helicopter	**H**OTEL
helmet	**h**ouse
hen	

Activities

Find the hammer.

Find the hidden hippo.

Count the hats.

Find all the helmets.

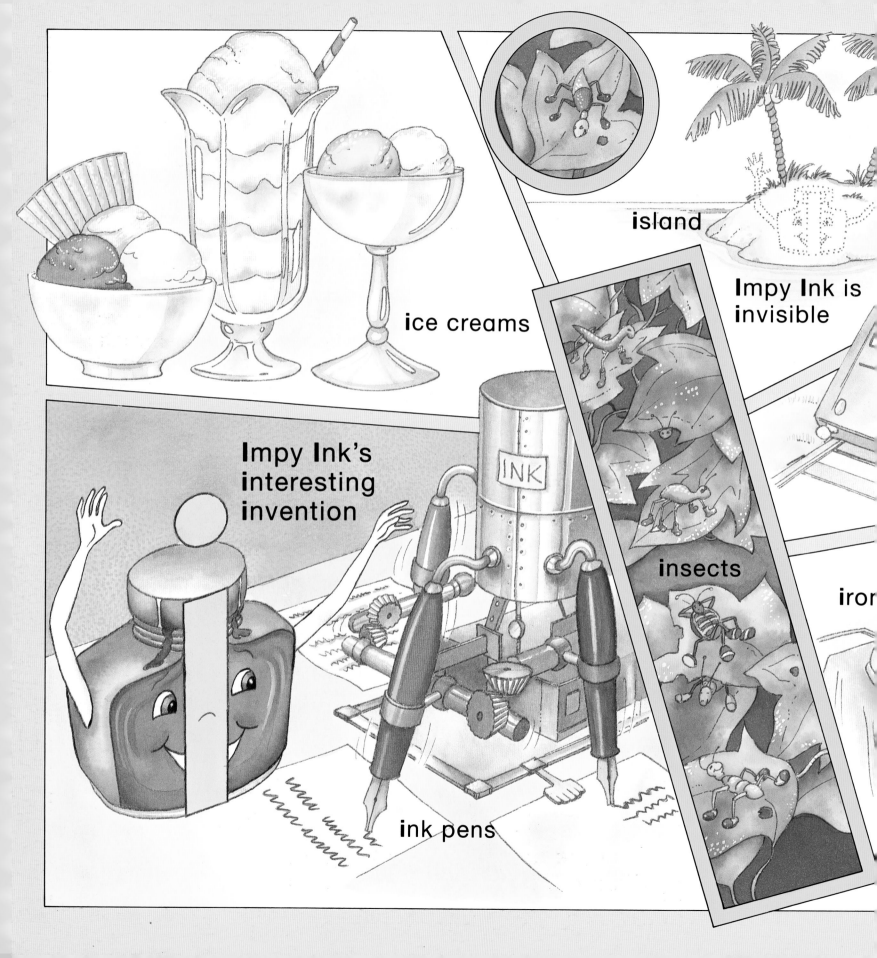

ice creams

island

Impy Ink is invisible

Impy Ink's interesting invention

insects

iron

ink pens

ill

igloo

intercity train

ice skating

invitation

Mr I the Ice Cream Man

Find the word

igloo	interesting
ill	invention
Impy	invisible
Ink	invitation
ink pens	is
insects	
intercity train	

Mr I
ice creams
ice skating
iron
island

Activities

Count the insects.

Count all the ice creams.

Find the invisible islander.

Jumbo **j**et

jelly
fish

jewels

jug

jeep

jaguars in
the **j**ungle

J j

Find the word

jacket	**j**igsaw
jaguars	**J**im
jam	**j**oke book
jars	**j**oker
jeans	**j**udge
jeep	**j**ug
jellies	**j**uggling
jelly	**J**umbo
jelly fish	**J**umping
jet	**j**umping
jewels	**j**ungle

Activities

Count the juggling balls.

Find the hidden jelly.

Find the jack-in-the-box.

kites

koala

kennel

Kevin

**Kicking King's
kites**

knigh...
knittin...

kitchen

kettle

ketchup

key

1 Kilometre to the Kingdom

kittens

kangaroos
kissing

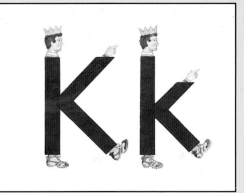

Kk

Find the word

kangaroos
kennel   **k**ingdom
ketchup   **k**issing
kettle   **k**itchen
Kevin   **k**ites
key   **k**ittens
Kicking   **kn**ight
King   **kn**itting
kilometre   **k**oala

Activities

Find two keys.

Count the kittens.

Count the kites.

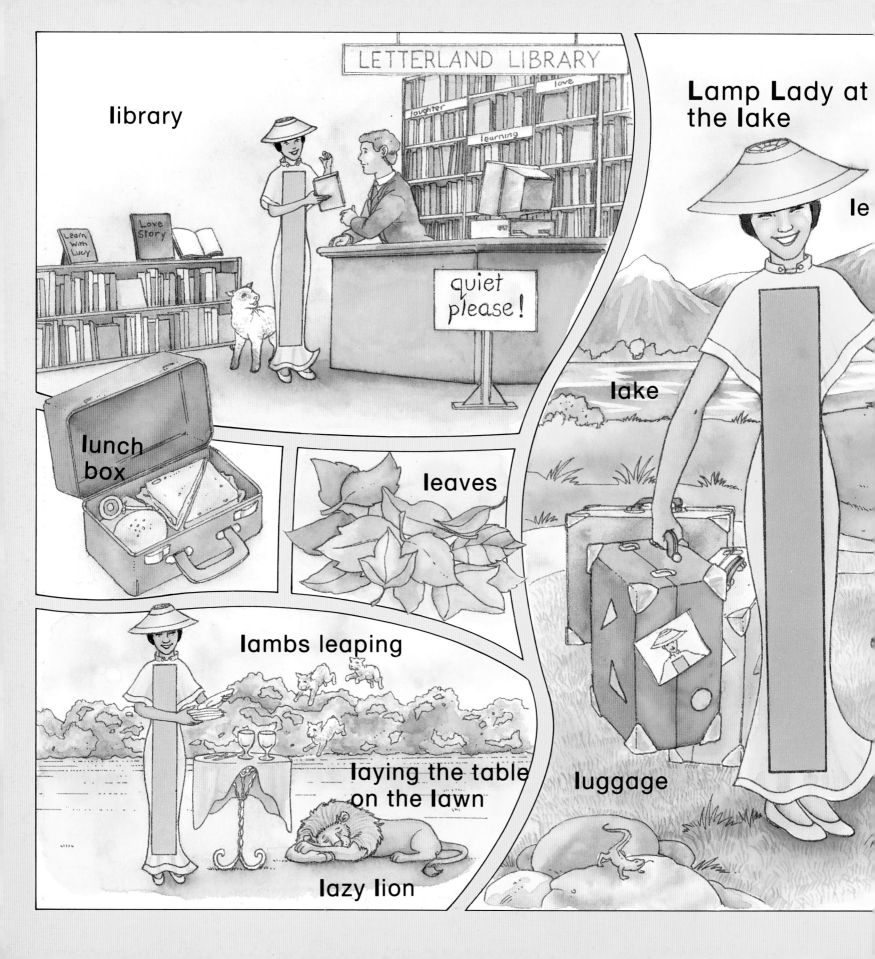

lemons

lightning

lighthouse

light
lunch
lettuce
lemon
lime juice

lesson

lifeboat

lorry

Len's Leeks

Find the word

ladder	lettuce
Lady	library
lake	lifeboat
lamb	light
Lamp	lighthouse
lawn	lightning
laying	lime
lazy	lion
leaves	logs
Leeks	lorry
lemon	luggage
Len	lunch box
lesson	
LETTERLAND	

Activities

Find the lizard.

Count all the lambs.

Look for a lollipop.

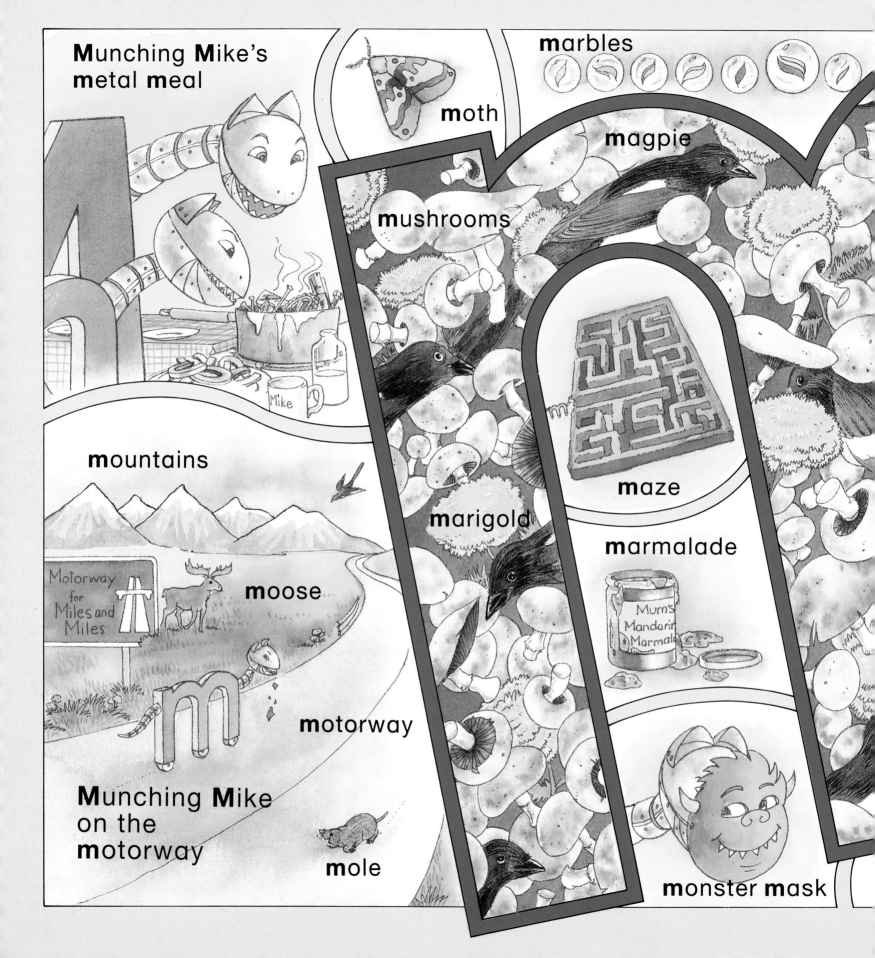

Munching **M**ike's
metal **m**eal

moth

marbles

magpie

mushrooms

mountains

moose

Motorway
for
Miles and
Miles

marigold

maze

marmalade

Mum's
Mandarin
Marmalade

motorway

Munching **M**ike
on the
motorway

mole

monster **m**ask

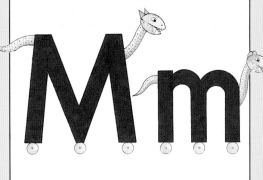

Mm

map

Motorway

Misty Mountains

Museum

Market

onkey

magic
mirror

model

microphone

music

motorbike

Find the word

magic	**m**odel
magpie	**m**ole
Mandarin	**m**onkey
map	**m**onster
marbles	**m**oose
marigold	**m**oth
market	**m**otorbike
marmalade	
mask	**m**otorway
maze	**m**ountains
meal	**M**um
metal	**M**unching
microphone	
Mike	**M**useum
Miles	**m**ushrooms
mirror	**m**usic
Misty	

Activities

Count the magpies.

What is in Munching
Mike's meal?

nest

No Entry

No Cycling

Notices

nightly News

No More Noise
say Nick's neighbours

number nine

Naughty Nick's
newspaper

noisy

neighbours

nails

needle

night

nurse

Find the word

nails	**n**ine
Naughty	**N**o
needle	**N**oise
neighbours	
nest	**n**oisy
net	**N**otices
News	**n**umber
newspaper	
Nick	**n**urse
night	**n**uts
nightly	

Activities

Find the hidden nightingale.

Add up all the nails.

Find the necklaces.

Count all the nests.

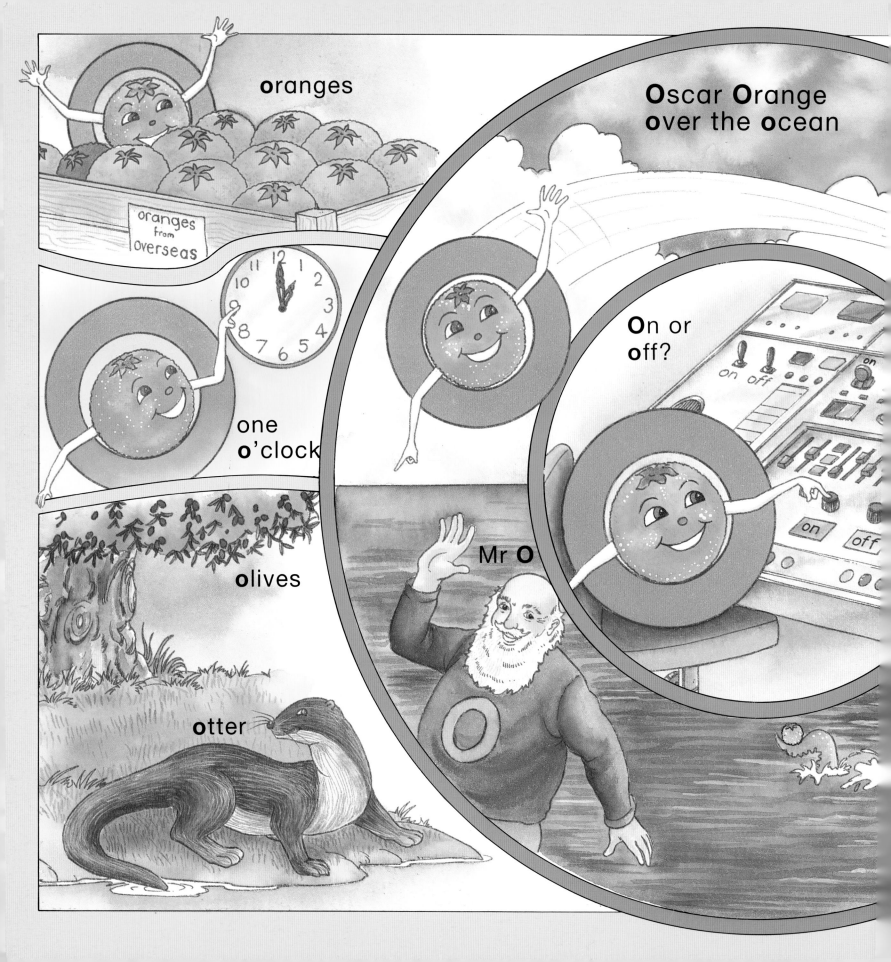

oranges

oranges from overseas

one **o**'clock

olives

otter

Oscar **O**range **o**ver the **o**cean

On or **o**ff?

on off

on

off

Mr **O**

octopus

office

Mr. O's office

open

ostrich

Find the word

octopus	**O**range
off	**o**ranges
office	**O**scar
olives	**o**strich
On	**o**tter
Mr **O**	**o**pen
ocean	**o**ver
o'clock	**o**verseas

Activities

Add up all the oranges.

How many legs on one octopus?

Which orange is the odd one out?

pencil

pennies

pears

Poor Peter and the postman

piano

penguins

postbox

postman with parcels

puddle

paws

palm trees

parrot

pirate

pig

poppies

picture

pupp
pain

urple **p**aint

pony

playground

pond

Private

picnic

policeman

paper

plane

panda

present

Pp

Find the word

paint	**p**ig
painting	**p**irate
palm trees	**p**lane
Pam	**p**layground
panda	**p**oliceman
paper	**p**ond
parcels	**p**ony
parrot	**P**oor
paws	**p**oppies
pears	**p**ostbox
pencil	**p**ostman
penguins	**p**resent
pennies	**P**rivate
Peter	**p**uddle
piano	**p**uppet
picnic	**p**urple
picture	

Activities

Find all the presents.

What are the penguins playing?

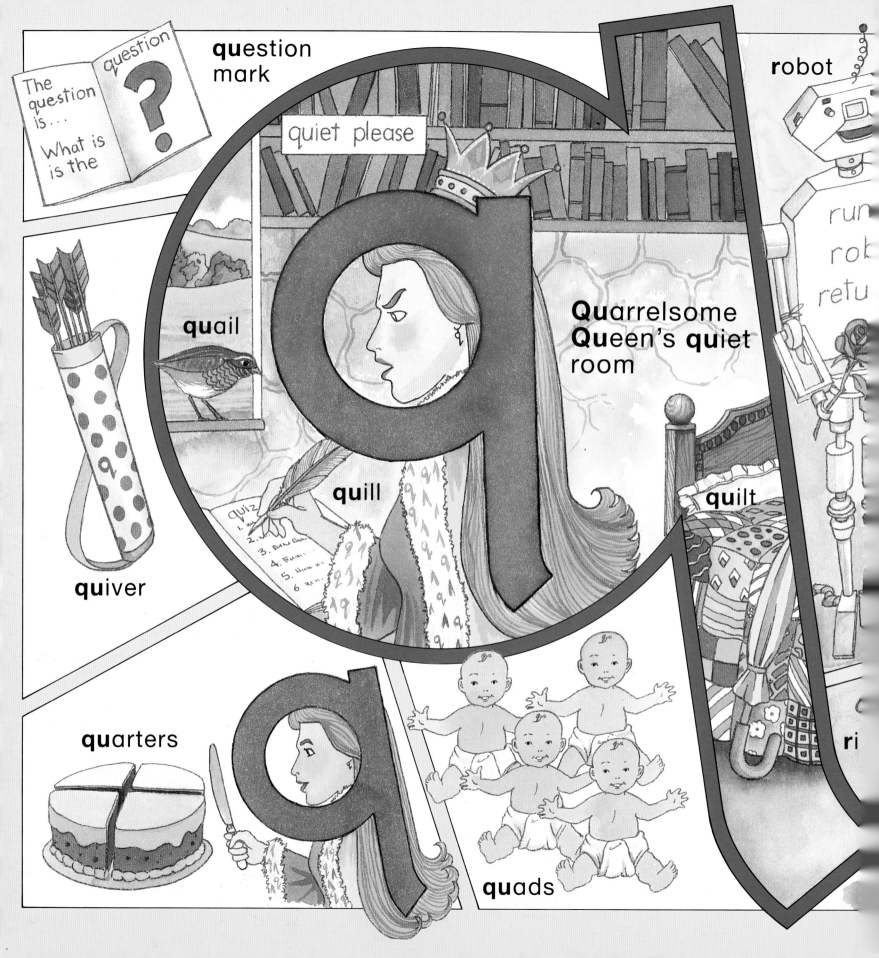

question mark

The question is... What is is the

quiet please

Quarrelsome **Qu**een's **qu**iet room

robot

run rob retu

quail

quill

quiver

quilt

quarters

quads

ri

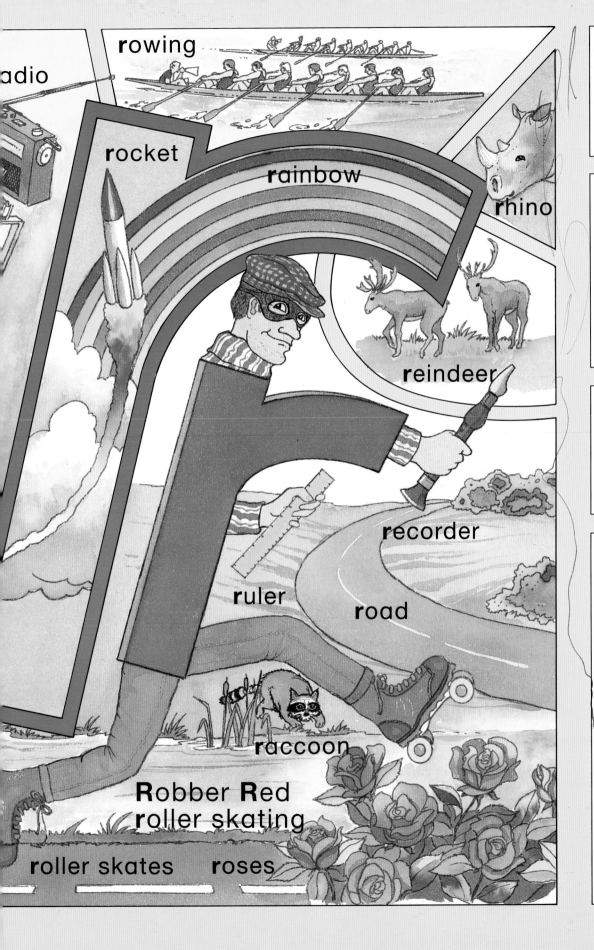

rowing

radio

rocket

rainbow

rhino

reindeer

recorder

ruler

road

raccoon

Robber Red
roller skating

roller skates   roses

Find the word

quads	**qu**iet
quail	**qu**ill
Quarrelsome	**Qu**een
quarters	**qu**ilt
question	**qu**iver

raccoon	**r**ob
radio	**R**obber
rainbow	**r**obot
recorder	**r**ocket
Red	**r**oller skates
reindeer	**r**ope
return	**r**oses
rhino	**r**owing
ring	**r**uler
road	**r**un

Activities

Find the reeds

Count the roses.

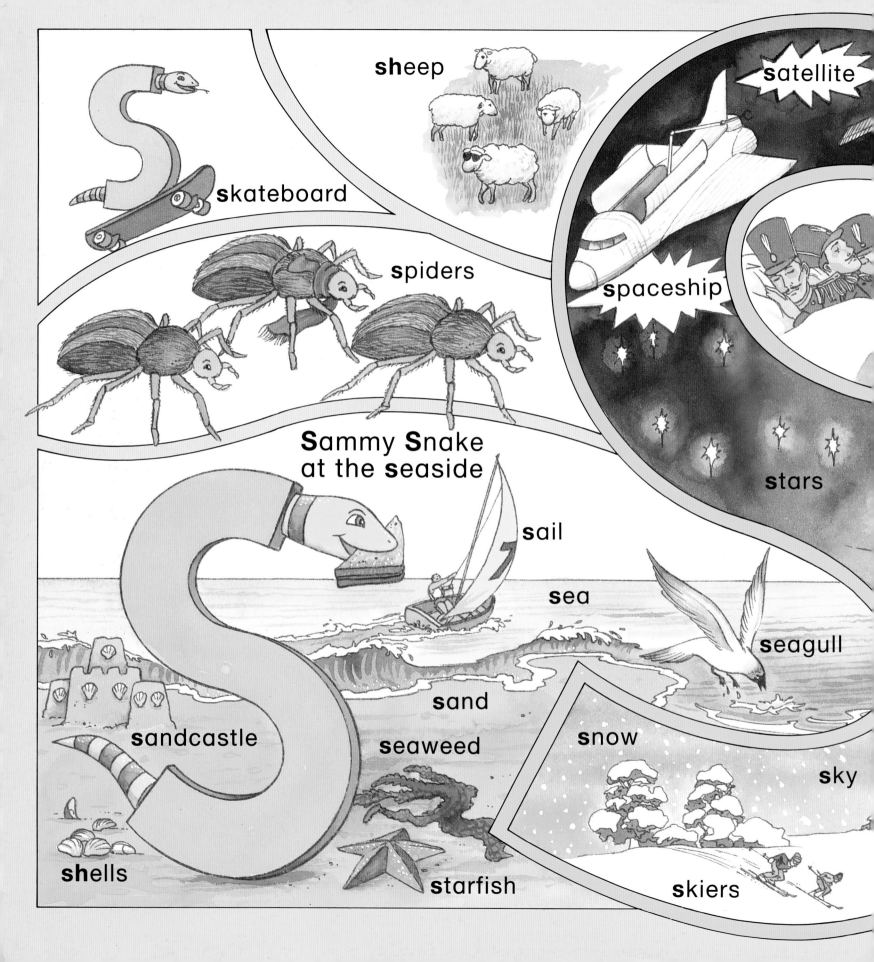

sheep

satellite

skateboard

spiders

spaceship

stars

Sammy **S**nake
at the **s**easide

sail

sea

seagull

sand

sandcastle

seaweed

snow

sky

shells

starfish

skiers

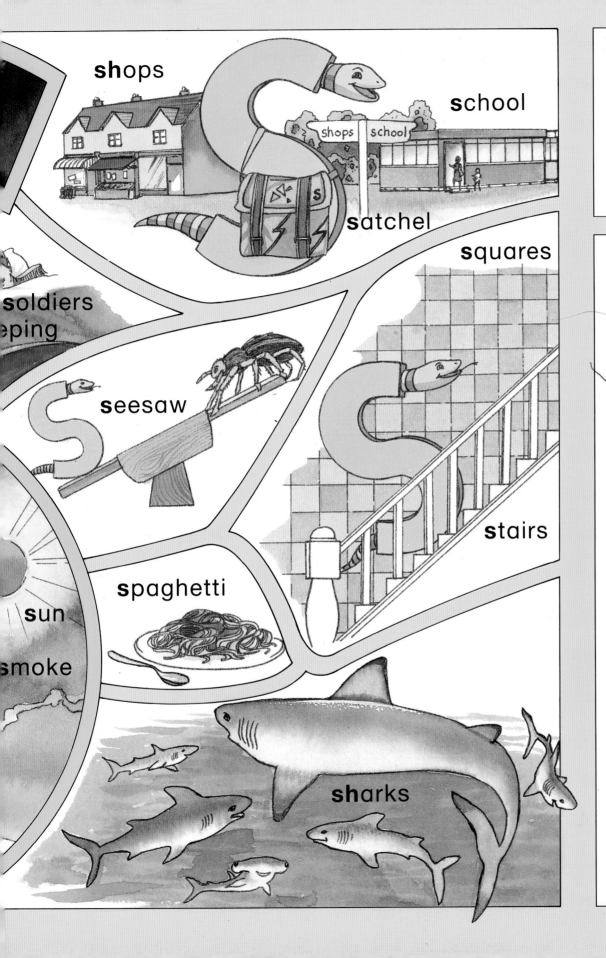

shops

school

satchel

squares

soldiers
sleeping

seesaw

stairs

spaghetti

sun

smoke

sharks

Ss

Find the word

sail	skateboard
Sammy	skiers
sand	sky
sandcastle	sleeping
satchel	smoke
satellite	Snake
school	snow
sea	soldiers
seagull	spaceship
seaside	spaghetti
seaweed	spiders
seesaw	squares
sharks	stairs
sheep	starfish
shells	stars
shops	sun
six	sword

Activities

Count the sharks.

Find the sword.

Add up all the stars.

tiger

train

two ter

taxi

toothbrush

tissue

tap

toothpaste

towel

tomatoes

television

typewrite

te
be

toys

Ticking **T**ess on
the **t**elephone

tape recorder

tortoise

ten tadpoles

trees

tractor

teapot

ble

tractor

target

Ticking Tom

toadstools

Find the word

table	toadstools
tadpoles	Tom
tap	tomatoes
tape recorder	
target	toothbrush
taxi	toothpaste
teapot	tortoise
teddy bear	
telephone	towel
television	toys
ten	tractor
tents	train
Tess	trees
Ticking	two
tiger	typewriter
tissue	

Activities

Count the tomatoes.

Find three tortoises.

Find the traffic lights.

Find the trampoline.

up

Uppy Umbrella
upstairs

unicorn

Mr U the
Uniform Man

unhappy

umpire

umbrellas

underneath

volcano

vulture with a violin

vines

viaduct

Vase of Violets

valley

Vet

visitors

Vegetables

Vince's Vegetables

To the village

van

Uu

Find the word

umbrellas	**u**p
umpire	**U**ppy
underneath	**u**pstairs
unhappy	

Mr **U**	**U**niform Man
unicorn	

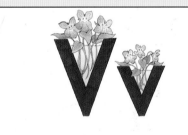

Find the word

valley	**V**ince
van	**v**ines
Vase	**v**iolets
Vegetables	**v**iolin
Vet	**v**isitors
viaduct	**v**olcano
village	**v**ulture

Activities

Add up the umbrellas.

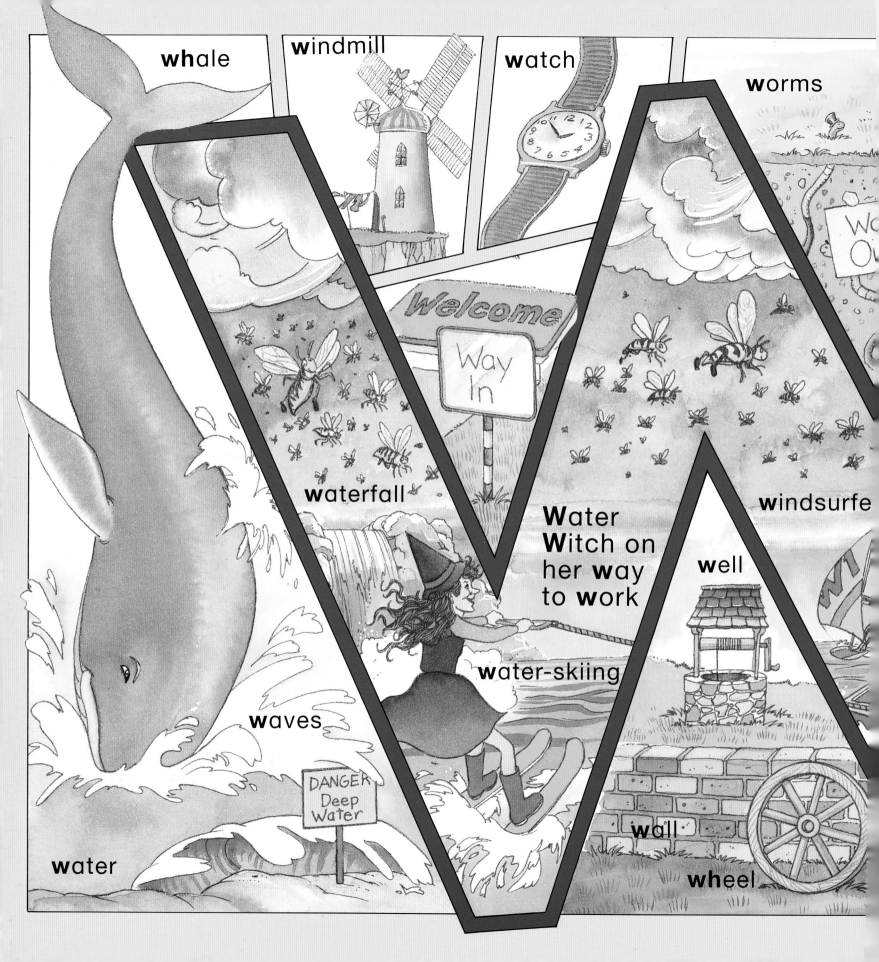

whale

windmill

watch

worms

waterfall

windsurfe[r]

Water **W**itch on her **w**ay to **w**ork

well

water-skiing

waves

DANGER Deep Water

Welcome

Way In

W[o] O[u]

water

wall

wheel

wood

wolf

wasps

washing machine

walrus

wool

wellington boots

Ww

Find the word

wall	Wet
walrus	whale
Wash	wheel
washing machine	
wasps	Wild
watch	windmill
Water	windsurfer
waterfall	Witch
water-skiing	
waves	wolf
way	wood
Way In	wool
Way Out	Woollies
Welcome	work
well	worms
wellington boots	

Activities

What is the Water Witch washing?

Who is the wolf waiting for?

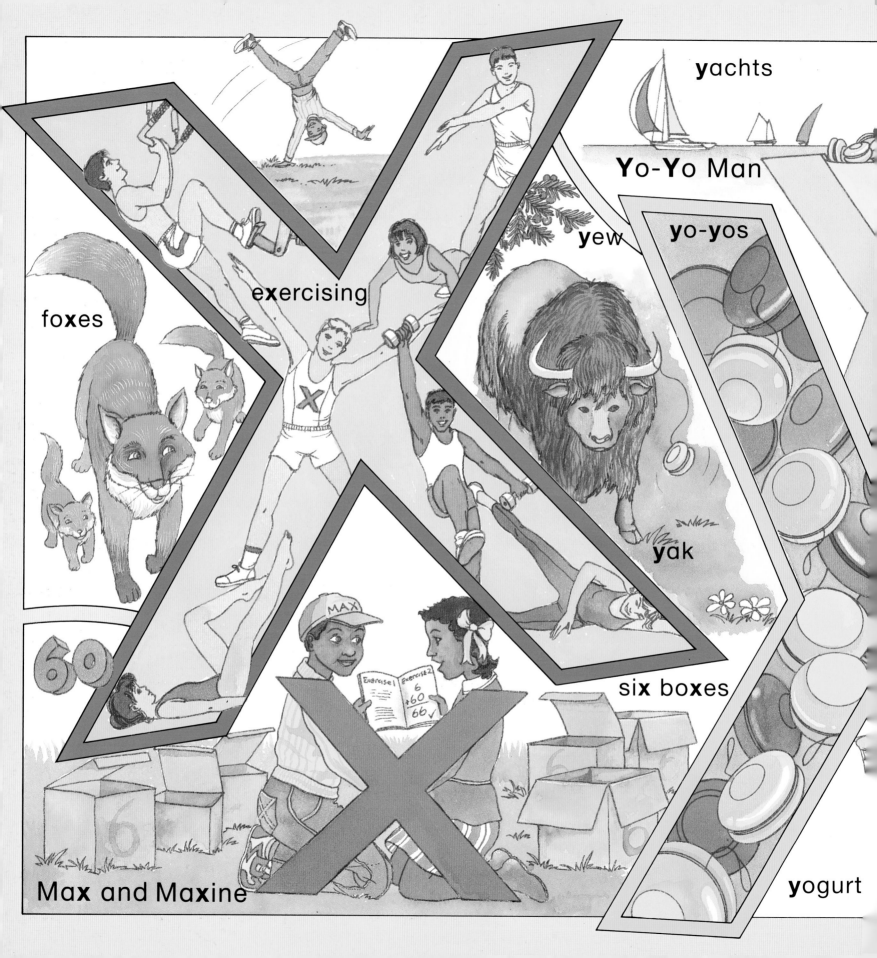

foxes

exercising

Max and Maxine

six boxes

yachts

Yo-Yo Man

yew

yo-yos

yak

yogurt

zoo

Zig
Zag
Zebra

zebra
crossing

zip

boxes   Max
exercising   Maxine
foxes   six

yachts   yo-yos
yak   yogurts
yew   Yo-Yo Man

Zebra   zoo
zebra crossing
Zig Zag   ZOOM!
zip

six lambs

seven Easter eggs

nine mushrooms

eight apples

ten bouncy balls

This book is dedicated to Alexander Carlisle – R.H.C.

Published by Collins Educational
An imprint of HarperCollins*Publishers* Ltd
77-85 Fulham Palace Road
London W6 8JB

www.**Collins**Education.com
On-line support for schools and colleges

© The Templar Company plc 1992

First published in hardback by Letterland Direct Limited 1992
This paperback edition published by Collins Educational 2000

ISBN 0 00 303477 1

10 9 8 7 6 5 4

LETTERLAND® is a registered trademark of Lyn Wendon.

British Library Cataloguing in Publication Data
A catalogue record for this book is available from the British Library.

Printed by
Printing Express, Hong Kong

www.**fire**and**water**.com
Visit the book lover's website